S0-ESD-180

Dyer's Thistle

Also By Peter Balakian

Father Fisheye (1979)
Sad Days of Light (1983)
Reply From Wilderness Island (1988)
Theodore Roethke's Far Fields (1989)

Limited Editions

Declaring Generations (1982)
Invisible Estate (1984)
The Oriental Rug (1986)

Dyer's Thistle

Poems by

Peter Balakian

Carnegie Mellon University Press
Pittsburgh 1996

Acknowledgments

These poems have appeared in the following magazines, sometimes in slightly different versions and sometimes under different titles.

Antaeus: "Last Days Painting (August, 1973)"
The Agni Review: "In Church," "The News," "Physicians"
Ararat: "Desire," Swallow's Castle"
Boulevard: "First Communion"
Illinois Review: "Saigon/New Jersey"
Kenyon Review: "American Dreaming"
Partisan Review: "Mandelstam in Armenia, 1930"
Ploughshares: "Home," "A Letter to Wallace Stevens"
Poetry: "The Oriental Rug," "Flat Sky of Summer," "A Toast," "The Color of Pomegranates"
Poetry East: "After the Survivors Are Gone"
The Southern Review: "Out of School"

"Rock 'n Roll" appeared in *Sweet Nothings: American Poets on Rock 'n Roll*, ed. Jim Elledge (Indiana University Press, 1994)

"Ocean," "Idyll," "The Backyard," in *Poems for a Small Planet: Contemporary American Nature Poetry*, ed. Pack and Parini, Middlebury College Press, 1993.

Immense thanks to Bruce Smith, Jack Wheatcroft, Agha Shahid Ali, Wendy Ranan; and to the Colgate University Research Council and to Alan Brown. My debt to Yaddo is on-going.

Publication of this book is supported by grants from the National Endowment for the Arts in Washington, D.C., a Federal agency, and from the Pennsylvania Council on the Arts.

Library of Congress Catalog Card Number 95-69473
ISBN 0-88748-232-5
ISBN 0-88748-233-3 Pbk.
Copyright © 1996 by Peter Balakian
All rights reserved
Printed and bound in the United States of America

10 9 8 7 6 5 4 3 2 1

Contents

1
- 11 Geese Flying Over Hamilton, New York
- 13 A Letter to Wallace Stevens
- 16 The End of the Reagan Era
- 17 Death-News
- 18 August Diary

2
- 25 Physicians
- 29 World War II
- 31 My Father on the Berengaria, 1925
- 32 The Oriental Rug
- 38 Duck 'n Cover, 1953
- 39 Flat Sky of Summer
- 42 Rock 'n Roll
- 43 Saigon/New Jersey
- 44 Out of School
- 45 First Communion
- 46 Woodstock
- 47 Last Days Painting (August, 1973)
- 50 Post Vietnam
- 51 American Dreaming
- 55 Mandelstam in Armenia, 1930
- 56 Swallow's Castle, Yerevan

3
- 59 The Back Yard
- 60 A Toast
- 61 The Color of Pomegranates
- 62 My Son Stares Into a Tulip
- 64 Idyll With Flying Things
- 66 Desire
- 67 The Morning News
- 69 In Church
- 74 After the Survivors Are Gone
- 75 Home
- 76 Ocean

Notes

For Helen

1

Geese Flying Over Hamilton, New York

That's how I woke
to a window of chalk sky

like indifference, like the sheet wrapped
around two people,

and the radio sounded like fuzz
on a boom mike,

the rhetoric needling in about the dead in Croatia

then the light came and the branch
of a sycamore on the wall
      was the menorah
on the arch of Titus

I was thinking like

the cows by the paddock in a peel of sun

when they cut a wide arrow
their feathers oily with tundra,
the gabbling like field-holler.

I looked out to the Fisher-Price toys
blue and yellow in fog,

silver light, gouache on the spruces,

and the words Pol Pot
the geese chromatic, then gone.

Phnom Penh static like snow the day may bring,
like a monsoon sweeping over a menorah

like the falling barn seeming to rise in white air.

When the spruces loose their shape
later in the purple air

my daughter will flick a switch,
and a stuffed chair will be a place for light to coalesce.

After dinner and a bottle of good Bordeaux
the sky floats like a numb pillow of radar.

Down here the dark is warm
like ordinary death.

A Letter to Wallace Stevens

1.

After the Reformation had settled the loamy soil
and the lettuce green fields of dollars,
the clouds drifted away, and light fell everywhere.
Even the snow bloomed and New Hampshire was a big peony.

A red barn shined on a hill
with scattered hemlocks and white pines
and the gates of all the picket fences were big shut-eyes.

2.

Sometime after the Civil War, the bronze wing of liberty
took off like the ribboning smoke of a Frick factory,
and all the citizens in towns from Stockbridge to Wilamette
ran wild on the 4th. The sound of piccolos lingered,
and the shiny nickel of the sun stood still before it
fizzed in the windshield of a Ford.
By then you were a lawyer.

3.

Charles Ives was a bandmaster in Danbury, and you didn't
give him the time of day. He played shortstop on the piano.
He never made it to his tonic homebase, and his half-tones
were like oak leaves slapping clapboard.

4.

How Miltonic are we anyway?

5.

In that red glass of the imagination,
in that tingling crystal of the chandelier
where light freezes in its own prism
and the apogee of the green lawns of New Haven
wane like Persian carpets in twilight,

there you saw a pitcher, perhaps from Delft,
next to a plate of mangoes.

6.

But, history is still a boomerang,
and the aborigines never threw one without a shield.

7.

Beyond the porches of Key West, beyond the bougainvillea,
your speech skipped on tepid waves,
was lapped and lapped by lovers and friends,
by scholars who loved romantic nights of the sun.

But the fruits and pendants, the colorful cloth
the dry palm fronds, and the fake voodoo wood
Cortés brought back as souvenirs
were just souvenirs. And the shacks and the cane and the
hacked plantain were tableaus,
and who saw them from your dark shore?

8.

The Protestant dinner plate is a segregated place,
where the steak hardens, and the peas
sit frightened in their corner while mashed potatoes ossify.
Some gin and ice cream and the terror of loneliness
goes for a while.

9.

As they say in the sunny climes,
abrazo.

The End of the Reagan Era

Endless horizons of wheat and corn
out of Willa Cather's reach,
and Ross Perot moving through it all.

I clicked a lever for my candidate,
the curtains opened like at Oz,
and my vote blew out the doors of the Jehovah's Witness hall.

I walked back through the saffrony maple leaves
just wet enough to stick to my basement trap door,
and sat outside and read some student papers on the Gulf War.

I thought of the states floating in their electoral colors
on the screen the way the scuds and patriots
flickered in their matrix dots before and after

the Giants played the Bills on channel 4.
In another century Galileo said "but still, it moves"
under his breath, and today the Vatican agrees.

Since legends keep us sane, I think today
of Cianfa, one of the five thieves of Florence
who was clasped by a six foot lizard

who ate his nuts and went right up his torso
until the two of them were two-in-one.

I love the clemency of roads this time of year
the way they tail off to the beautiful barns.

Death-News

When I pick up the phone
it's like the Bay of Bengal
lapping in the perforated plastic.

There's wind in the jackpines,
cones are scattered and remind me
of black mitres after Lent.

Silver silos, flaking barns, black-faced
whites, route 20, four miles north
of my house, cuts past dairy-bars

half-painted ladies, hotels
for Tony Perkins, vinyl houses
with wooden signs, 'antiques.'

The sky is ploughed
and furrows are speckled white.
Red kernels stud the oaks

and hail assaults the tin roof
of the porch, and by noon it's rain
and smells of thaw, so the arms recall

July. Then snow squalls blot
out dusk and the heart's a tire
in mud. My daughter races in,

her hair the color of Moroccan olives.
From the knot of circuits,
and the byzantine April sky,

there are plastic holes
sweating in my hand,
and then a voice.

August Diary

8/1

From here groomed fields and clumps of trees,
a silo of corrugated tin and a white barn blur.

Unseasonable cool days,
high, blue, a few clouds like ripped pillows
as if this were a lip of the North Sea

and I could look out and imagine Denmark.
But I'm in my office three floors up.

8/3

In Armenian there's a word—*garud*—rhymes with hood.

The beautiful ones are not faithful
and the faithful ones are not beautiful—

a student said that about some Pavese translations,
here in my office.

Should I tell you what *garud* means?

8/5

What's happening in Spitak and Sarajevo and the West Bank
is splayed like the cortex of a silicon chip in the fuzzy air.

Marina, the physician from Armenia, was 25 & had one plastic arm
and one real arm. I met her in East Hampton on the deck of a
             house on the dunes.
After the earthquake she had no husband,
no parents, and only one child.

"I'm in a good mood today," she said, "let's talk about

something else." I poured her an Amstel Light.

8/10

The coolness intrudes—
month of wind-sprints and retching for the coach.
It comes back like nerve ends after surgery.

Along a country road cicadas rattling.
Chicory and sweet pea intruding on the ripe barley.

I picked up some seed packs from a junk shop on Rt. 20,
a tomato blazed in red ink/1926, Fredonia, N.Y.

8/11

What's between us? The red ink of the tomato?

How does an image stay? Or is it always aftermath?
The way deep black reflected the most light in Talbot's first
                                          calotypes.

But *garud*: tongue of a snake,
meaning exile, longing for home.

Thomas Wedgwood got images by getting sunlight
to pass through them onto paper brushed with silver nitrite:

wings of a dragonfly, the spine of an oak leaf—
fugitive photograms. But he couldn't stop the sun
until it turned the paper black.

Stop the light before it goes too far?

Or is desire what *garud* means?
Longing for a native place.

8/17

Marina said she was learning how to connect nerve-endings
in the hand so hands and arms would work again.
There were so many in Armenia without working hands and arms.

At the end of each dendrite is a blurred line
like the horizon I'm squinting.

Image of the other:
light-arrested; not the image of ourselves.

8/21

After digging scallions one day Dickinson defined freedom:
captivity's consciousness, so's liberty.

Maybe *garud* is about the longing for the native place
between two selves.

8/22

I love the brute force of silence in Roger Fenton's
Sebastopol from Cathcart's Hill, 1855. The Crimean inner war.

The artlessness of silver is like my tongue in your wet space,
or like the news photos that bring us the pressure of disaster.

Beloved topography,
Garud then must mean yearning.

Is that how we loved under the rattling Nippon porcelain,
in the light calotyped by the fire escape?

8/25

garud: the grain chute that spills
into a dark barn which is endless,

like the self when it's out of reach.

Are we that lonely that a constellation
could blacken and fill up that same barn,

and that be us?

But still we're piss and oats and stock in there.
We're like civet; who wouldn't love it?

8/31

Salzman said about new glass plate pictures:
they're as transparent as air, like windows

with the fragmentary, scruffy particularity
of real living behind them—

2

Physicians

1

Above school kids in Episcopal
jackets cherubs are singing
to the beautiful fake lapis
of St. John the Divine

and from this side chapel
I see through the blue
to the 6th floor of St. Luke's
where my father's heart caved in.

In the thirties my grandfather
made his rounds three floors down.
In the weak sun the black rocks
by a shepherd's robe seem piled

like fat medical texts
or small suitcases full of Dickens
in German, my grandfather translated
to learn English so he could pass

his exam in the Empire state,
to use his silver instruments
on the eyes ears nose and throat.

In a snapshot he's large-eyed, glazed,
as if he should've followed
his cousin, the Archbishop, to a cave.

Instead he climbed down
the catastrophes of New World
faces, the warped shapes
that flare up the senses.

Tubes lit in the throat.
The auscultated fog
of the ear tuned
to pass the pitches

of the world. I think of him
scoping the cochlea,
that purgatory
where the screech

of a yellow Checker
and the mute twittering
of Satchmo's horn
were white light.

Down the ducts of joy and pain
my grandfather called tears
(not lachrymae Christi),
but the fissure between two continents

that sent him with Armenia's
refugees along the junked canals,
the Dardanelles, the Atlantic.

Eye to eye with a lens,
he could see the retina's
orange spot,
and it was a floating nation.

On a clean metal table
the empty whites stared back,
like marbles flickering

in Turkish moonlight.
The piles of Armenian corpses
he tended in Adana he carried
in the tremor of his hand.

2

A dark plane slicing Zurburan's pears.
The ripe light in the bell-end
of Cezanne's pear strokes,

the honey-colored vials
weighing down a tree of life.
My father pointed these out in museums.

But in that pear-shaped organ
from which the raucous parrots flew,
in that fruit of blood

soaking in the vaults of the chest,
my father worked.

If you could loose your love to flow
down there in the eddies that swell and shrink

against the barnacled and moss-spun bulkheads
you would see the contradictions
in the oscillations of the unstillable red sea.

Amidst envelopes of membranes
venous trunks and a splay
of filaments which wire a pump to the head,

my father could be a man of adamant
tying his terror in a Windsor knot,
pressing it to the icy starch of his shirt.

I could tell on certain days he'd felt
the inward suck,
the vortex where men and women disappear.

In the final seconds, he'd say,
'the heart's a bag of worms,
then it's all calm,'

and slipped into his formal chair
distant as blue light;
asked for salt and bread
and water without ice.

World War II

My mother worked
for Irvington Varnish
south of Newark where
her sister lived

in a room writing
like Katherine Anne Porter.
My mother wore goggles
and a white coat

to earn college tuition.
In Budapest Eichmann mulled
over 200 tons of tea,
2,000 cases of soap;

Jews for supplies.
My mother was gloved past
her wrists rigging
polyester for parachutes.

The shadow of a poplar
on the wall was the hand
of the Turkish wind.
My grandmother feared

my mother would disappear
into the brick buildings
of the college catalog.
Topf & Sons made vans

in '43, and the waste
was slight as it slid
into the Bug River.
Bucknell University

was a dark copse
past the Delaware Water Gap
where Turkish gendarmes
emerged in the daylight.

My mother boxed khaki
and flint, and a hand
placed electrodes on
my grandmother's head,

while the grackles
in Upper Silesia ate
powdery ash on the oaks.

Ions: a convulsive seizure,
ECT they called it,
and my aunt slept on
a *Ship of Fools* in a run-

down room in Belmar.
On cool sheets in the evening
when the poplar shadow
disappeared, my grandmother rested

and my mother returned
from work, when the sun
on the oil drums of the Pike
was pure acetyline

like a road out of Armenia,
out of Turkey, out of Treblinka,
out of New Jersey.

My Father on the Berengaria, 1925

The sky like the red silk of the fortune teller
in Bucharest. Diesel fuel.
Things rise here.

The letters flying like swans on the passport
Republique d'Armenie. I've never been there,
is it a country?

Gulls squawk into the dirty sun.
A refugee is a free person.
Mother said "yes, yes."

She said "when the lights go out,
don't be afraid, we're here."
And the train rocked like the wind had arms,

over the trellised rumbles,
over the olive grove and the wool and garlic.

Constantinople floated away like the sun
on cups of waves the color of pee.

In the shade of the Arc de Triomphe
we had cones of lemon ice.
"There's more of that in New York."

When I crawl through the wet cotton
and the hemp and leather of the hull
I smell Lucia's hair in my room.

Dark air is the inside of a brass urn.
I have the neck of a swan in my hand.
I'm twine. I'm breathing.

The Oriental Rug

I

I napped in the pile
of the brushed and bruised
Kashan on our living room floor

an eight year old sleeping

in vegetable dyes—
roots and berries,
tubers, shafts, dry leaves

the prongy soil
of my grandparents' world:
eastern Turkey, once Armenia.

The wine-red palmettes
puckered with apricot buds
and fine threads of green
curling stem-like over my cheek

leaving a shadow like filigree
on my eye as I closed it.

The splintering green wool
bled from juniper berries
seemed to seep, even then,

into the wasp-nest cells
breathing in their tubular ways
inside my ear and further back.

*

On certain nights
when the rain thrummed
against the clapboard

and my father's snoring issued
down the hall
I slept on the rug
curled and uncovered

and the sea of ivory
between the flowers
undulated as if the backs
of heavy sheep were breathing
in my mouth.

The prickly cypress
down by the friezed border
spiraled in my night gazing.
Armenian green:

dwarf cabbage, shaded cedar,
poppy stem, the mossy pillow
where my grandfather
sat in the morning dark

staring at the few goats
that walked around the carnage.
Outside my house the grass
never had such color.

II

Now I undo the loops
of yarn I rested my head on.
Under each flower
a tufted pile loosens.

I feel the wool give way
as if six centuries of feet
had worn it back to the hard
earth floor it was made to cover.

Six centuries of Turkish heels
on my spine-dyed back:
madder, genista, sumac—
one skin color in the soil.

I lose myself
in a flawed henna plant
jutting toward the scroll.
Its rose-pink eyes burst

off the stems.
The auburn dust
which reddens the women
returns with a sharp wind.

The vine of lily-blossoms winding
by the fringe once shined
like fur when a spray of sun
flushed through a curtain—

that gracious shape hardens now
like a waxy twig at summer's end.

I hear wind running
through heart strings.

I hear an untuned zither
plucked by a peacock's accidental strut.

Warp and weft come undone;
sludge spills back to the earth

(my liver's bitter
as the pomegranate's acid seed).

III

The heavy mallet a Parsee boy
once used to beat the knots
beneath the pile so
the weft would disappear

vibrates in me
as the knelling bells
over the Sea of Marmara
once rang toward the civilized West.

I pitch myself,
as into a waterfall,
into the spinning corolla
of an unnamed flower

coral, red, terra-cotta,
and tangle in its lattice of leaves
and follow lines

from my palms
to the dark balm
of the marshy hillsides

of my far away land—
the poppied acres
of Adoian's hands.

IV

I pry my way
into a rose—
undoing its blighted cliché.

I strain for the symmetry
of its inflorescence,

slide along the smooth
cup of a petal
till I rush head-first
down the pistil

feeling the tuby walls
muscle me to the ovary
where a bee is swooning
on some pollen.

Wrapped this tight
I suck my way into the nectaries;
feel a hummingbird's tongue
and the chalky wing of a moth.

That wet, I wash
to the cool leaflets,
rim their toothed edges,
then back-rub

the remains of sepals
which kept the rose alive
in blighted April
when Adana and Van were lopped
off the map.

I come apart in the thorn—
(the spiky side that kept the jackal out)
and disperse whatever is left
of me to the downward pull
of cells sobbing in the earth.

V

I walk with a rug on my back.
Become to myself a barren land.
Dust from the knots
fills my arms

which in the peaceful new world sun
becomes fine spume.

A sick herbalist
wandering in a century
mapped by nations wandering.

The dyes come through the wool,
break the grid of threads
holding the shapes to form:

safflower, my Dyer's Thistle,
carry me on your burr
so I may always feel
dry gusts on my neck.

Kermes, dried like a scab,
crush me to your womanly scarlet chest.
I feel your scales
flutter in my eyes.

Madder root—
which makes the red of Karabagh
bleed along one long hallway.

Tyrian purple, from a mollusk shell
lodged in Phoenician sand—
gurgle all your passion in my ear.

for my daughter, Sophia

Duck 'n Cover, 1953

A shadow of a bough
hangs on the wall like a headless mutt.
Tic Tac Toe of the windows,
then maples like gold lamps.

We start with "My country 'tis of thee,"
and end with the Lord our Shepherd.
Out of the light blue
that siren makes us deaf.

Kimshee makes my father sick.

We know what to do.
We don't stumble on a shoe,
or move our pencils from the beveled grooves.

The nap of my crew-cut bristles my knees.
I look at shoes and the shadows of leaves.

The light spills like a brook
into the seams of rocks.

Korea's a sky-blue thumb on our map above the kitchen sink.
The floor boards shine like honey.

Patent leather. Saddles. Bucks. Buster Browns.
There's a saying that passes among us like water,
put your head between your legs and kiss your ass goodbye.

The Y in my alphabet soup floated toward the Yalu.

Then we sit again on our maple chairs
bright as yellow-jackets.

Flat Sky of Summer

In a salt-rutted
scooped out side of a dune,
I curled around a picture book,
skinny and burnt brown as a beetle.

Staring through the glare
of the midday sun,
hot enough to scatter
my puffy white friends,

I thumbed those pages
in the rank wind
like a slow boy
learning to read.

I dropped down
a Minoan bowl;
drew into the gray and red
folds of its coil

rested on the dry
thumb-rubbed bottom
hearing water splash.

In the sandstone of Ur
bits of shell
laid-in purple rock,

or the curly headed
straight nosed boy
playing his double flute

to the berry-winged bushes
in the tan silence
of a wall in Tarquinia

chalk and dust
on my tongue.

*

In the chips of gold (more real to me
than the science fiction of Revelations),
in the nimbus over the pear-shaped head
of Christ—a sun within a sun
on the high lunette of Holy Wisdom,
beyond the hammers of Iconoclasts,

in the flat gold-leaf sky
of the Armenian past
on vellum the color of sheep's milk
where a teal bird,
a green twig in its beak,
flew out at me,

I felt a twitter in the visible world.
The ocean stilled each ripple
to a cup of light
in the perishing peachy sun.

*

The half globe of a breast
caressed by the shadow of an odalisque.
Almond dust on Sephardic eyes,

a thigh of broken light
scattering Modigliani's head,

the petals of Vincent's tongue
drying in the windless heat of Aix,

the sun needling the poplars,
Ucello's lancers soaring

in the quills of hawks and eagles
above the pressure of the wind;

off diaphanous plumes of white
a breeze of turpentine
apricots and cherries bleeding
on the Gorky green world,

a magenta iris blooming in the stomach,
snails and worms crawling
in the blood's sugary sediment;

out of the sand brown ground on my hands
a butter churn, a clay baking tub,
the Kazak's sun-cured scarlet,

and where the lavender trees grew out
of the lake's white salt
I saw the heraldic branches in the yellow light
of Toros Roslin's mind—

the humming beehive of the testicles
the spinning albumen of the ovaries
the rouge lips wetly on the white dove
flying between my legs.

Rock 'n Roll

The groove in black vinyl got deeper—

What was that light?

A migrant
I slid into a scat,

and in the purple silk
and the *Canoe*

there was sleekness and a rear-view mirror.

And the Angels flew out of the cloisonné vase.
They were the rachitic forks hanging in the midnight kitchen.
And so I called you after the house was still.
My turquoise Zenith melting

and you asked: what was that light?

I was spinning. I was the trees shivering,
and the snake of coiled light on the ceiling
was moonglow.

I wasn't a fool in a satin tux.
I was Persian gold and blue chenille,
I was the son of the Black Dog of Fate.

I said: I saw a rainbow of glass
above the Oritani Theater.

Lord, lead me from Hackensack New Jersey
into the white streak of exhaust.

Saigon/New Jersey

It was russet light, Orchard Lane,
white-shingle colonials

and the ch ch of the sprinklers,
small rainbows in twilight,

the fabric-smell
of funeral parlor on us.

From a fence we fell
to the fairway on all fours,

a sky of purple berries,
and my hand swollen from a doubleheader,

Ho Chi Minh, a tin sound in the air.

A brash oak casket
was less than the absence

of your brother's arm still clear
as the ghostly rubber of the mound.

Your Heaven Scent heavy
as we slid into the trap,

and the white number of the flag
grew incandescent. You who loved

the classics said Orion's eyes
were wild birds against pure black,

and our bodies burned
into each other.

Out of School

When the cheerleaders faded
and the oaks were stripped

Sunday was a worn sky
in which a ball was blunt

as a faded moon, austere like
going steady. A text unglued

and names and dates crammed
in drudgery fell out. Carthage

was desolate, and Caesar humped
his polished legions past the Rhone.

On the winding bands of Trajan's
column the Parthians were screwed

to the foul mouth of posterity,
felicitas saeculi—

bits of color flickered
on the ceiling of my room,

and Dylan's a cappella rose
through curlicues of smoke

over the college flags
of *veritas* on the wall.

I listened till my ear was numb
and the face of Hattie Carol

was black wax like those horses
turning into history.

First Communion

Mother of God. The wine lusted
on my lips. Weeks and weeks
in the world.

It was a rainy morning in May.
The forget-me-nots still powder blue,
odorless, clean with yellow eyes.

I stood outside the closed curtain.
The ceiling hung like a chalice
of air.

I knelt in wet clothes
and a cloud rose over me.
Ashes. Myrrh. The oblations.

Without deceit or wiles the rain
came in sheets, blurring the windows
to a place without doors.

Woodstock

In the mud of a tire rut,
    we were the filaments.

We said if Mrs. Agnew could make music
    on Spiro's flute

we said the clubs in the hands of the Chicago cops
    would liquify.

The trees shook with the throb of steel.

What did we do to be so red, white, and blue?

We were inexorable
    like the dialectic unravelling from Hanoi
        to the Jacksonian grass.

We were the inebriates of vitamin C and cocaine,
the daughters of the gray flannel suit.

And when the shaman spread his yellow robe like the sun
he was all teeth and amp

and what were we?

Last Days Painting
(August 1973)

The plain air above the Palisades,
the blue anonymous egg,

can you make chromos by electric light?

I couldn't tell sun from stone
        Tenafly's varnished light
from the rambles around Hoboken—

*for instance Lancon, Lemud, Daumier, Gavarni
and Bodmer remind one more of piano playing.
Millet is perhaps a solemn organ.*

Against the static clouds,
a gull in the bourbon light—

a nude descending,
the sky comes to its knees on the rocks,
and if the things that emerge

are black and gray
and if the unpretentious gulls fly into them
I could be chalk.

Descending: surveillance of the visible
like Nixon, and the face caught on
the horizontal band of the old Magnavox.

You could say that somewhere between
Masaccio and Alexander Portnoy is the truth.
I lost my head up there

in a satiny roundel, like the sun's pucker.
I wanted to make the crêpe de Chine
of her slip into a cloud

unravelling in summer rain
so she could really fly.
Descending: Watergate, denouement, worm's eye.

*I envy the Japanese the extreme clearness
which everything has in their work, simple as breathing.*

*

Can't trust what's in a tube.
Take gum resin from a plum tree.
Cut it up, put it in an earthenware pot

add water and put in the sun.
Stir carefully, strain through a cloth and grind
all pigments with it. Saffron: from the dried stigma

of a crocus. Theophilus used the pigment for making tin look
like gold, but clear yellow glass too.
That's what I wanted. Clear yellow glass,

so that things could be seen like the steel
of a Chevy in the cement and iron of the
collapsed West Side Highway,

or the rusty light gleaming
from the sterns of the Cunard liners
in the filthy harbor;

it's why I believed in Heade;
his canvas as if the world were a glass
dish, silvered by an amalgam

let down into the well until it grazed
the surface of something
and everything came back like a raised ornament:

trees, rocks, a boy, a canoe, a straw hat.
Heade's America: Vietnam reversed.
Fifty years hence nobody will wish to go back

*to this period, or if there follows a time
of antiquated decay or so-called
'time of perukes and crinolines,'*

*people will be too dull to think about
it at all; if there comes a change for the better tant mieux.*

*

If you look at van der Weyden's sky
behind the cross, it's a void.
A place of the Buddha, as if our inspiration

reflex were reversed and the self
imploding with nothingness could see.

Today I'm a bright casualty
on the verge of something new
as when desire marries the skyline,

clean, and unaugmented, like the hem
of God's robe—where the world
is no longer the tooth of a gargoyle.

Go there.

Post Vietnam

Hecuba

Did I nurse for nothing?
Were my women too wild
when they combed their bracelets
on Polymester's face?

I stalked MacArthur till
his slate face sank in the Yalu.
Saw Westmoreland lose an eye at Da Nang.

From my burnt-out sockets
I see Botha's car
crystal clear as a Caddy.

Andromache

I used to watch the crows,
like dads and lads in the trees
of their countries.

I used to genuflect,
now I'm custard.

The iron wheel's Hector's head.

I've split for a place
north of Tonkin,

my breasts
are Venetian glass.

American Dreaming

1

I rowed through rushes.
Root-knees and loops
barely breathing,

maggots lisping,
bubbles breaking.

Spikes and bristles brushed
my arms,
and the reeds' pith split,

and spindles of air rose.

2

Heard a foot in sludge—

a sound like an Armenian word.

3

At Sandy Hook,
the lighthouse spoked the air,
as if wicks still burned
in spermacetti.

In the wave-washed paths
of lobsterbacks,
in the reservoir of blood-money

Hessian smoke
thinned to ciphers

The tower of junkstone stood
in the empire's sediment.

Fog wrapped my head.
The light was straight
as a gull's wing cutting the air

and water slid like a black eel
through weirs and hooks of grass,

and the sounds of familiar names

Hackensack, Ho-Ho-Kus, Fort Lee
Passaic, Engle wood, Tena kill

lodged in a channeled whelk.

A thud of European muskets
in the air,

and memory's a sieve for Delaware skulls
to pour like powder.

As the flint-heads
were swallowed by the waves,

I saw the white,
scarless, fog-wrapped beach

and the shreds of breech cloth
unstitched from Pontiac's flag

beneath the plastic cups
from the luncheonettes and beach vendors.

4

In the stench of chub heads
and the trailing skirts of air,
my gaze

gave way to Armenian silt—
the cradle in the crook'd
neck of the Tigris

where a crone rowed
out of a corset
into the pleated reeds:

the linen stiff with sun
on the sandstone like parchment
in a silent place.

In the rice's chiming pale
a black partridge ruffled
water in the conch
of my ear.

Lost tea and filaments of silk
settled in my throat.

Shrunken beds,
once Armenian trade routes,
were fissures in the palm.

Corpses floated
like bloated goat skin.

Apricots dried to ears.
Almonds blanched
to eyes.

5

As the moonlight parted fog,
the way the sun shifts

steam in a Turkish bath,
that scouring light glittered
on black water,

and the air
was a broadsword.

I watched the light
rinse the surface
and diminish like the white string of a kite.

I rowed back to the bulrushes
imagining their slick piths
were candlewicks

holding my two waters together.

Mandelstam in Armenia, 1930

Between arid houses and crooked streets
a shadow could be your wife or a corpse
and a mule's hooves sounded like Stalin's
fat fingers drumming a table.

In the Caucasus eagles and hawks
hung in the blue's basilica.
A swallow flew off a socle
into the wing of an echo—

history's caw and chirp and bird shit
on the tombs in the high grass.
On hairy serrated stems,
poppies flagged like tongues!

Petals of flat paper
lined your thumbed-out pockets.
Anther seeds burned your pen.

From a cloud of broom a red bee stumbled,
to your fish-globe brain.
A casket of honey-colored light
kissed the eyebrows of a tree.

Lake Sevan's rippling blue skirt
lapped you. Slime tongues got your eyes.
A half-dead perch slithered your ear.

When the evening air settled
on the creatures of the mountain
the sun was an ovum
or the Virgin's head.

Here, where the bush grew with fresh blood
and ancient thorns, you picked the rose
without scissors. Became an omen.

Swallow's Castle, Yerevan
(Armenian Genocide Memorial)

I came to a place set into red tufa,
where poplars tremeloed with birds,
and gullies spilled down the hills.

I walked with a twin-needled obelisk
in my eye, and thirteen slabs of obsidian
leaned toward the center.

From the throat of Gomidas,
a raspy flame.

I stood in that circle,
felt the glass edge.

Let Noah's vine wither
to a strangler's rope,

the sky fill with billows of bombazine,

the heart
's a bag of paper in the wind.

3

The Back Yard

Out of blueness,
the hummingbird in the privet.
Then silence
shafts the sky:

and you can hear
a cat yawning,
missiles moving to Griffiss,
a scarf of chartreuse
drying like a caterpillar.

The seeds in the heart
are like plovers lost inland.
Don't try flying with them.
Just feel the lift,
and the horizon

is the color of raspberries
fermenting in the shed.

But then the hummingbird's gone
and the air is a flask
for the henna-tulips . . .

coils of amber
powder down the shaft
as if they've spilled from a white rose
breaking up in the wind . . .

and neither a twig
nor the obelisk of a birch
can measure a distance.

A Toast

A branch smooth as the rubbed foot of St. Peter,
puce, porous, rinsed by wind.
Clean spear of a skeleton.
Bridge of a Roman nose.
Cask of air.

When I walk into that croft,
the trees at my back like a reredos
carved by rain,

then the day could pour like ouzo
into my crystal thimble—
a shot of air for friendship,
a bar of bleached light
for the necklace of stones
strung on the chalky ridges—
a blackbird smearing the trees
for our daughters in the alizarin of day.

Then, a swallow could hook
its neck on a rafter,
a hawk mistake a lure
for God and Country

I wouldn't know—
my shot glass
a splintered flock of feathers
in the wind.

for Bruce Smith

The Color of Pomegranates

The hills bunch on an empty page.
A shade of rouge on a woman's cheek.

All day I've walked the streets of Capuya
where the sun was a flute on fire
burnishing a brown river.

Pink and blue bed sheets flapped in the wind.
The daily bread was fresh with light,

and the trellised grapes of the terraced
mountains hung like vases.

If one could etch in wine,
think of the white horizon!

But the streets are narrow and crooked
and take me down to the river

with goats who pick at rubbish
and live in stones and weeds.

At my back the hills are distant,
some red sand leaves dust on the page.

My Son Stares Into a Tulip

He was nuzzling
in the grass I had just cut.
Crushed bluebells on his palms.

He nudged a few inches
like a caterpillar or something amphibious
and then caught by accident

his hand on the ha-ha,
and so braced his pale, slightly bowed legs,
to bring himself upright

for the first time, I think,
in his life,

and found himself face to face
with a tulip, which was falling

apart from a week of sun
and a recent harsh shower,

and so its black stain
was like sticky dye.

I watched him stare into it.

In the house his mother's
breasts were drying up
like the crabapples of September.

If words could fill the
gap in his life
each petal would become a tongue,

each black anther
a stalk of light.

I hope his upright grasp
of the green stem holds him
when he's fallen back to ground.

I hope a breeze descends
on him from the blue.

Idyll With Flying Things

I lived behind a window
shaped like a peony
and when the chickadees
flew into the evening,
I thought they were bats
because they twitched
when they flew too close
to telephone wires

and veered from light
thrown in crosses
by the far-off city.

I wiped the mullions
with Fantastik.
Sat down, got up,
walked around.

When it began to rain
I called a handyman
to caulk a hole in the joist.

I wore Oxford buttondowns
with thin stripes
and shaved before the sun
was too high.

For a few hours my face
took the light,
and the chickadees came

and I caught a view
of a flag torn by light,

the saucer lip of a stadium,
and a glass skyline—

the sky was
the iridescent back
of a Japanese beetle.
The sun thickened

like old varnish
and the reed-slashed meadowlands
rose up, beyond which I could see

Desire

Cattleya in a jar of water,
a door opens.

A bee alights on the lip,
vermillion   shut-eye.

Still water   no glass,
the throat is dirt.

The heart   goes up   in air.

The Morning News

Through a glass door
    a pheasant grousing the snow,
through the maples

a Baptist spire
    in the blue Adirondack sun.
Purring from the Krups.

On my wall a small map of the flat earth
    Hic Dragones; an open mouth
of cobalt like terra incognita.

I think of Elizabeth Bishop's map:
    raspberry, shadowed green
exotic peasants like *the moony Eskimo*

and the conceit of countries
    Norway's hare
spills into the furrows of laid paper.

My son who is 1
    waddles in like a drunk
in his blue corduroys

presses a button:
crominance, luminence, syncronization:

a shadow mask. Phosphors:
    green   red   blue

The Berlin wall
    is a dam of people.
The windows of a split-level

in east Belfast blown-out.
    A woman, a teen-ager
really, slips into jeans

tight as silk on her ass;
    then a bottle of beer
frothing over the shaft.

A man in a dull suit
    goes on reading a cue
about bottles found inside

the throats of farmers
    as my son
tripping pulls the plug.

Then my daughter flings open
    the sliding glass door.
A little meadow of snow

glistens then melts into her hair
    which is the color
of Smyrna figs.

She runs to the TV
    puts the plug in
a new station comes up.

In Church

1

In the rheumatic heat of July,
when Public Enemy blared
on the blasters

in a time when arbitrage
and foreign policy
were bureaus of each other,

I made a wrong turn off Broadway
and wound up at St. John the Divine

where I sat in the hot dark
until the traffic died.

*

And a voice comes over
some columns to the breeze of the Golden Horn
over the cypress groves

and flowing bougainvillea
where the bright blue weather and the old
sea walls come together,

where crates of cardamom
and musk are piled and
the cattle hang in blood

above the brass,
where the grain boats
stink and red pleasure-

barges drift where Jason
sailed for his fleece—
a voice comes out of the dead water.

In Hagia Sophia
light pours in rosy bars
on the porphyry and the green marble

till the air blooms,
and a chrysalis of lit crosses
makes circles in the air.

Light falls through the lunettes
like arrows of gold that could've
snuck up the Virgin's dress.

Had the Holy Ghost flitted in
it would've been lost in the glare

and the kiss of peace
Justinian blew from the ambo.

*

Incantations flutter and rhyme
in the apse like gentle wings
in a cloud of incense

thinning on the gold-leafed
vaults where the tongue's vibration
lingers in the upper air,

and rises and rises as if the dome could open
to a half-hemisphere of heaven
where in the translucent glitter of the Kingdom

the Saints are poised in gracious robes
with their thousand year frozen faces—
the one truth glued on the grout of their lips.

2

I sit with the incense of memory,
and a bath of dark pours
from the vaults above the pew.

Outside boutiques of money collide
with the street fires in Harlem, whole
skyscrapers are levitated by arbitrage,

and the only inside takeover I can negotiate
is myself in this pew with my herringbone jacket
which I should chuck in the Salvation Army bin

down the block, so I could join the line of choir
boys in their last innocent ritual
as they stand before the mounted sermon sign

"he shall bring forth judgement unto truth"
(Isaiah 42:3). The Puritans, because
they believed God's altar needs not their polish,

lifted the boulder of truth higher than the glittering
face of the Nazarene once leaded in glass.

For the spirit they swallowed stones
and shattered all the panes. But beneath the lavender
arch of a Canon Table in an old Gospel

I once tasted the consubstantial dew drop
in the faded color of a peacock's wing.

So while a stone sinks to the bottom of my
river, a peacock's wing floats by the shore.

Who tells it like it is: Isaiah or Procopius?

3

I started walking backward
down the aisle

when I heard and thought I
saw in the strange venestration
of that light,

a voice,
first incoherent, and then sharp
as if it were in my ear

*There is no reign that executes
justice and judgement;
is that why you whine?*

'But Primo Levi's image of a man—
a face that haunts every nation
on the earth—

this, this!'

Don't soak lentils in your mouth.

'Be serious; what's left to praise?'

*The fig tree drops rocks
in the morning and the fig
tree drops figs in the morning.*

*It's your new yard, am I right?
New house, 2 kids, and all that.'*

'Yup.'

*When a Santa Ana blows fire down the coast
do you run to meet it in a leisure suit
or with a silicon chip?*

*Does a squirrel stash nuts
of self-pity up its ass?*

What are verses for?

And the raisin light dribbling
in the clerestory faded,
and it was cold

as I backed down the aisle:

'We'll talk more when you're off duty.'

After the Survivors Are Gone

I tried to imagine the Vilna ghetto,
to see a persimmon tree after the flash at Nagasaki.
Because my own tree had been hacked,
I tried to kiss the lips of Armenia.

At the table and the altar
we said some words written ages ago.
Have we settled for just the wine and bread,
for candles lit and snuffed?

Let us remember how the law has failed us.
Let us remember the child naked,
waiting to be shot on a bright day
with tulips blooming around the ditch.

We shall not forget the earth,
the artifact, the particular song,
the dirt of an idiom—
things that stick in the ear.

Home

When you're in the mountains
you feel the desert air.
Waking to fog on a salt marsh
you taste the empty boulevards of July.

The earth shifts with you,
one road hooks to another—
a travesty of coins, shards of an amphora,
a trail of carnelian,
things to palm at a riverbend.

Words in the hand are a solidus
of cadences, or a little pyramid
of topaz in the shuffled dust of the *souk*
and the sky's the iridescent eye
of an open peacock.

Lines chink like bronze and copper wares
wrapped in newspaper,
pummeled in a suitcase,
stashed under the seat.

When you get alone
where the border is absolved
by a horizon,
open your suitcase

unravel the newspaper,
and the green patina
will crawl out onto land
like thick skins of rust.

Home is where water turns to air
and submerges the cities.

Ocean

Out of her salt hips
poured my umbel.

My mouth full of shells
and her tongue
a lemon bristling my teeth.

Foam flowered
and the black grapes
tasted sweet again.

I smelled fenugreek,
the cherry pit's talcum,
cod drying like a sandy slipper.

An amaryllis opened
in my throat,

and the pain issued
toward the islands.

Notes

The End of the Reagan Era
Cianfa: from Dante's *Inferno*, Canto XXV

Physicians:

Adana: province in south central Turkey where 50,000 Armenians were massacred in April 1909 by the Turkish government. This was a precursor to the 1915 Genocide in which the Turkish government exterminated 1.5 million Armenians, who were living on their historic homeland of 3,000 years, and deported another million Armenians, thus wiping out all Armenian civilization in Anatolia. My grandfather worked as a physician for the Armenian victims in Adana in April 1909.

The Oriental Rug:

Kashan: floral Persian rug
madder: herb yiedling red dye
genista: spiny shrub yielding yellow dye
Marmara: sea between Asiatic and European Turkey
Adoian: family name of painter Arshile Gorky, who was born in the
 Armenian province of Van
Van: Armenian province in eastern Turkey
Karabagh: mountainous region of Armenia famous for its long-rugs

Flat Sky of Summer:

Kazak: a colorful, bold, geometric rug, indigenous to Armenia and the
 western Caucasus
Toros Roslin: 13th century Armenian manuscript illuminator.

Last Days Painting:
lines in italics are from Van Gogh's letters

Mandelstam in Armenia, 1930:

Stalin exiled Mandelstam, for writing an allegedly seditious poem, to a life in labor camps. In 1930 Mandelstam was granted a respite and went to Armenia where he wrote his well-known essay "Journey to Armenia," which broke his writer's block.

Swallow's Castle, Yerevan

Gomidas: Armenian composer, musicologist, and priest, who went insane after witnessing atrocities of the 1915 Genocide.